In Which I Play the Runaway

Rochelle Hurt

In Which I Play the Runaway

Rochelle Hurt

Barrow Street Press
New York City

Designed by Robert Drummond
Cover painting by Steve Kim,
    lullabyspring (3)

Published 2016 by Barrow Street, Inc., a not-for-profit
(501) (c) 3) corporation. All contributions are tax deductible.
Distributed by:
    Barrow Street Books
    P.O. Box 1558
    Kingston, RI 02881

Barrow Street Books are also distributed by Small Press Distribution,
SPD, 1341 Seventh Street Berkeley, CA 94710-1409, spd@spdbooks.org;
(510) 524-1668, (800) 869-7553 (Toll-free within the US); amazon.com;
Ingram Periodicals Inc., 1240 Heil Quaker Blvd, PO Box 7000,
La Vergne TN 37086-700 (615) 213-3574; and Armadillo & Co.,
7310 S. La Cienega Blvd, Inglewood, CA 90302, (310) 693-6061.

Special thanks to the University of Rhode Island English Department
and especially the PhD Program in English, 60 Upper College Road,
Swan 114, Kingston, RI 02881, (401) 874-5931, which provides
valuable in-kind support, including graduate and undergraduate interns.

First Edition

Library of Congress Control Number: 2016951732

ISBN 978-0-9973184-2-5

for my family and all the elsewheres

CONTENTS

I love the I,
frail between its flitches, its hard ground
and hard sky, it soars between them
like the soul that rushes, back and forth,
between the mother and father.

—Sharon Olds

Some place where there isn't any trouble.
Do you suppose there is such a place, Toto?
There must be.

—Dorothy Gale

Last Chance, California

Poem in Which I Play the Runaway

It could open with a party, strewn
with girls like tinsel, girls looking
for a house to stuff themselves in,
girls with two parents, girls glaring
with the joy of needlessness.

Or a chase scene: some ranch house
with walls thin as a mother's dress,
long emptied of men and closing on me.

I never wanted a home in him,
but the sex was like licking sheets
of corrugated iron, my torn maw
breathing in the corrosion. The scent
of him alone was like coming
home to a father's midnight grip.

In this way, I was forever
the runaway, indolent trinket of his.

But if you want it, I'll give
the story of a woman's deboning
by a pair of junk-rutted hands,
her good marrow honed to a prick
on a promise like a diamond file.

And how she loved it, the sin itself
a new kind of homelessness.

Dorothy Tries

What pilgrim shadows—
how stubbornly they tail you,
children better left at home.

The tawny stalker slinks, sour
puss following that silver marauder—
always after your heart, girl.

You are dragging
yourselves toward paradise:
one brick, one brick.

By now your feet are swollen
to the size of pomegranates,
pulsing fuchsia inside

hand-me-down pumps.
They'll callous your feet in no time.
How cheap you look. And how long

can you carry this limp
man, throat full of straw, all impotence
and good intentions. *If I could*

find my heart in here, you say
to the world, searching
your basket, *I could make it love you.*

But all you find inside
is the little ashen dog
drooling on the sandwiches.

Self-portrait in Neverstill, Oregon

Mornings here, I take half-measures
of gin like medicine—in nervous teaspoons

that clink like wedding rings, a sad tune
set to the metronome of kitchen counter fingernails

ticking down the days. I've lived a hundred years
inside this hissing kettle of a house, singing

to the boxcar beat of his feet coming home
to me: a wood-step shuffle. In tinnitus dreams,

crickets trill themselves into me, tiny screws
turning. Every morning, I dig another

note from my ear. Every night, I open
his mouth, and we drown them there.

Letter from Aunt Em

Dot, you won't know what you're in for
here until you're choking on it, straw-
throated, and all those mistakes

squirreled into your cheeks—fat face
of regret, the face of your mother, looming
drunk and shrunken as a week-old birthday balloon.

Think of the women you could be. Then think
of me.
        Fill yourself up before you come back.
Fill yourself to breaking with breath.

Self-portrait in Last Chance, California

Dusk is it—the certain forever
hanging heavy, heavier.
                        You're here,
so you feel you must take certain measures—

stucco the sky before the clouds dry, blot
the oily catkins oozing from the alders,

collect the bees left woozy from holding
their electric breath above the shivering
grass,
            where the gummy dark of time spreads out
around your too-small tennis shoes, untied.

But look around—the light has been let out
            like air from a balloon.
                                    Quickmud, the black
ground slips further from you.

The grass moves, remembering wind.

How to hush its hundred bloodless seedhearts,
wheezing in the soil beneath
you, pregnant with regrets?
                        Water pours
            into the far-remembered meadow
of your childhood, and there are your parents,

dog-paddling toward you, pinching their mouths
into terrible Os, ugly as hatchlings.

They want so badly to tell you, to tell you—
but only the gurgling suck of drainage breaks through.

How did they get so old?
                              Night is a clot
gathering behind the eye, dark little platelets
scabbing the sky.
                    There is no seeing past this.

You'd be smart to leave now, dreamless.
Best to pile the bees on the sidewalk, release
the unloved weeds.
                    In this garden, babies
blossom then rot, quick as magnolias around you
and indecision's perennial sprouts
crowd your mouth as silence blooms and blooms.

Bad Luck

The first time my mother learned how lightning loved her, it came through our TV. The light reached out and cupped her breasts, holding her for a minute before spilling into her belly, which lit up like a bulb. That's when we saw it—something curled there, stone-still, like a child carried too long. I called it regret, but my sister said she didn't believe in such sentimental things.

We watched my father's touch grow brittle after that, chipping little by little against my mother's cheeks, and withdrawing completely after the second storm, when light soaked through her hair in gray swaths and painted her fingernails white as eggshells. It became hard to say who in our house was more haunted.

I was tapped twice: on the shoulder, on the hip, a finger of light. Twice it pulled me out like a fish from the ice, and twice I was thrown back to my body, a cradle of bone. I told my sister that it felt like a sudden loosening, a seal opening somewhere inside me. Then that familiar tickle of liquid seeping down my thigh, like life sieving right through me. She said I shouldn't tell such stories.

But only after my daughter was struck, and walked out of it as out of a lake—resplendent, blinking the static from her eye, shaking drops of lightning off her tiny hands—were we certain. Conductivity, the textbooks called it, the easiest path down to the earth. Bad luck is what my father said—to be loved by a force like that. Every storm was a prayer, then silence, a fear of last words in the air. Eventually, he left us. My sister, too—for the desert. I wasn't surprised when my own husband vanished, terrified or simply tired of sharing his bed with our brand of death. You could smell it like smoke on our breath.

My mother's skin had become translucent, and I could see a clearing burned inside her where regret used to sit. It was then I understood a woman's body as a bowl, open to whatever may fall into it. But loss is a choice, she said, to become the haunt you've run from.

Hurt, Virginia

Self-portrait in Hurt, Virginia

I was born a fleck of mill trash
bedded in a black hill, a cry
stoppered with crabgrass.

I lived as a stick in the stuck-mud
drift of land called Virginia.

I was born among a clutter of cats
and tongues sloughing a crust of coal-spit
from their coal-bit teeth.

I was born an apology.

I was born with a gift for gall and grit,
late to a woman with hands
as slick as her knickers.

I was born a breadcrumb in a trail
of fathers leading out of our clapboard house.

I was patched into a tawdry dress
my sister wore for prayers and hollers
until it was torn from her hips

and a kernel of a baby shook loose,
my sister's skin wrapped around his like a noose.

You'll never tell home from hurt,
my father said. His kiss was a curse
placed on my mother's forehead.

Music Box

As you hum, a tiny room unfolds
from the papered wall. Inside, all
    you remember of her: a cinder doll;
teeth from a burst bone comb, scattered
    like pine needles across the floor;
an onionskin record sleeve, trembling.
    Charred chair frames rise like pines
from the flame-scraped carpet, forest
    green, and a trail of string
leads back to a finger, worm-curled
    inside the womb of a deeper room. You
peer further into the mouth of the wall:
    a thumb—for thumb-sucking it was
that day that made your mother storm
    from her stove, leaving the fire
to lick at the cotton rag like a dog, leading
    to the eager spark and lurch
of flames you heard as your mother rushed
    from the washroom with a bar of soap,
stopped, and turned. Through the tiny hall,
    a squall of flame skims your eye, giant
at the mouse hole. Ear up now, dear,
    to hear the bottle of breath uncorked
and swallowed in one sorrowful gulp.
    Ear up to the cusp of your mother's lip
like a door to a mouth slamming shut.

Self-portrait in Only, Tennessee

Tell me how he held his gun, girl—the only
grip steady enough to lift your skirt
by the same angle your stepfather worked
the day he pointed your mother's face to the sky,
anchored you on his back, and left her
neck craned in prayer, mouth cocked,
their only baby suckling the bullet inside.

The only conclusion you could come to
about Tennessee men: don't let them
touch you, a lesson learned only after
that first pretty boy pushed through—
he like an auger, and you with that hole

in your icy chest, from which any number
of slippery dreams could be pulled, gutted,
and slapped in the skillet to hiss beneath
the wooden spoons of your mother, despairing
in their pitcher on your lonely stove—your only
son born like a beautiful scab on the wound.

Dorothy and Uncle Henry

Lone Ranger on the radio, sullen
ghost of your mother shooting
puffs of smoke through her nose,
while outside the fields are full of pennies
and screams—it's Halloween,
and Uncle Henry is juiced.
He's a fan of the cowman
too, he tells you during a dinner
of fish sticks and beans. He spits
a *hi-yo* as he angles his legs, cocks
one hip and tosses his fist, invisible
rope over your aunt, a sack
of drunken laughter on the floor.
Wanna skin her, he jokes
as he holds her arm out
to you in your buccaneer costume,
prod and rein limp in your palm.
He thinks you have something
to prove, too. *Kiddo*, he says.
He thinks he'll win you.
But he doesn't know you
are counting his steps, licking
your cowlick with vinegar,
twining his grin into a noose.

Self-portrait in Aimwell, Alabama

Some words can kill: our mother's insistence—
so aim well. A regular bluff: nightly we find her
with the untouched rifle sleeping like a baby
at her breast. Gently, it snores and trembles
with breath, remembering my father's fingers
on its neck. A lifetime ago, she folded herself
like a paper napkin into his palm.

                                    In our house now,
a constant echo: quiet crumpling from our throats.
In your hands, Daddy, our origami hearts pleat
infinitely. Faithful to our mother's advice, we hide
words like bullets under our tongues, repeating
only the one that must have lodged in her spine
before we were born—*love*, our aim
ever fixed on our father's eyes.

Diorama of a Fire

In the living room, evidence
        of accident: glue dropped

on the floor, welling with the glare
        of the steel nail scissors, giant

beside the candy box sofa. See, propped
        on top, two horse-haired dolls.

See their fixed elbows, greased with heat. See,
        stuffed in this one's hand, a linen scrap—

my sister dabbing at my knee, stirring
        the gravel trapped beneath

the plastic flap of sallow skin.
                           What care,
to weave these bits of glass and rock
        and grass into the flesh of the knee.

Left of the paper partition a moth lies
        folded—my mother—soot shoulders
                curled, face taut as she falls

        infinitely further inward

and her shoebox house coughs up gray bolls
        of cotton, pasted to the walls around her.

But the spark is further back.
                   I sift
        the stack of cut-out colors—the black

chain of smoke, the orange match head,
      the brown shred of flooring—and find

at my fingers another white rag, paper
      edges scalloped, cloud-round.
                                  I remember
it into the cardboard kitchen, where it sits
      stoveside, doused in peroxide, dripping.

      Now watch: I am a godhand
pulling loose threads from the curtains,
      testing the corners with breath.

Self-portrait in Nightmute, Alaska

Winter smears the horizon with silt and the days drop
to us like shrunken plums. This is when tongues grow heavy

in their toothy caves. Call it instinct. Call it shame. Either way,
I slip rocks into my pockets before I go out. Just in case.

In the schoolyard, buzzards hover and boys on bikes
sew a circle in the sleet around me. They stitch their names

into my skirt, say *baby*, they know me—in parentless rooms
where my name unravels at my ankles, and crumbs of words

fall away from my face. They don't bother with blinds
or curtains, so the sky is a scold as the stars glare down at me,

and the tide mimics my shunted breathing. Walking home
past Our Lady of Perpetual Help, silence swells and fog

closes like a mouth around me.
                                        Sister, I am a song
swallowed. Marring the black, the houses are orange,

furious with light. Inside, you are sucking smoke
from the lit tip of a Marlboro wedged in the teeth of man

I don't know. You welcome his shadow into your throat
like a gag. But later, when you hit the wall, you ring like a bell,

a symphony of tongues clashing inside. I try to remember
to close my door the next time he unfolds you

like an old tablecloth, shaking the other men out, leaving
his name like a grease stain. Unzip one day, and find another

waiting like an old coat of paint, same shade. The morning
sun is a lie through the window as we fry our silent eggs inside

the din of the Westminster Chimes, the light etching us in two
tones like an old photo, our matching mouths scratched out.

Dorothy as the Lone Ranger

He's the quintessential reinvention: self-
serving secret avenger, perpetual runaway.

But little foundling, you'll never stay
gone. Em once said if you'd been born
elsewhere—on a mountain, a mansion, a horse—
you might have a father, a dollar, a dog
with a brain. But what for, on these plains.

The straw hair, the oiled skin, the fleas
and pigeon toes, those salami dressed
in red—what did you think you had
waiting? Next time, you tell yourself,
a mask will be your saving.

Halfhearted

Some women marry houses. / It's another kind of skin
                                                    —Anne Sexton

The older women always told me gold lies in men—an alchemy of flesh into currency, a melting down of sex into a husband into a baby into a mansion. So I made sure love hitched me to a duplex: two is better than one, right?

The ladies were onto something about the gold, at least: from two men, I got two wedding rings. As a married woman, I slept in two different sides of a building split by a wall like a spine—a necessary bilateral divide. I arranged the furniture in each half to mirror the other, and the house became a perfectly symmetrical organism. To stay faithful, I never let my two husbands touch the same parts of me. I severed myself into half-breaths, half-laughs, half-peeks. Three days a week I lived in the right side of my body, dragging my left leg behind me. On three other days, I lived in the left, carrying my right arm against my chest like an infant. I seemed to be perpetually winking, and my husbands were never sure which of my words should be taken seriously. This kept them on their toes, always waiting to see more of me—though in truth, there was no more coming for either one of them. See, love split me open like a ripe nectarine and each half began to decay in its own way. No man could suture my skin back into longing.

But here's where I got a break: on the seventh day of each week I lived in the pit of myself. Houseless, husbandless, I slept outside, balanced on a rock—tough, whole, unable to be consumed by any desire. On those nights I was happy.

Needmore, Indiana

Self-portrait in Needmore, Indiana

As expected, after the wedding, the house
became a cough we lived in, trembling
in the throat of that asthmatic spring.

The streets stacked and curved like fingers
on a grease-knuckled hand gripping
the waist of our Midwestern dream.

We went sun-blind inside just looking
at each other.
               Death is not working—
but wanting—too hard. My father's body
was little more than a paper bag by the day
he died and tumbled into a graveyard.

I could have died etching my name
into the glass eye of my cage—a bay
window painted with lace. The skyline
in its expanse was a farce played out each night.

Sometimes my reflection was the star
of the show. Sometimes it was the child
clapping from her seat, so looking out
and looking in became the same thing.
Sometimes it just rained for weeks.

Infants of the Field

*Stories of rescuers finding small children alive after tornadoes
have carted them off have become so common as to seem
apocryphal.* —Patrik Jonsson, *Christian Science Monitor*

The wind has wanted to keep you as promised things,
captured and slung from the trees like giftling skins

on the hunting rack in the yard, your fathers' animal
anger for all to see, a heap of sour evenings—

mothers trapped like starlings, wanting the world
through a window, thinking of how a creek behind a house

always looks cheap like cellophane with the knowledge
that it dries up a mile down. No one has loved you

like the earth in its lupine fits, its precious jaw, steel hinge
of wind, the vapor tongue—only wanting to raise you

by the necks from your mire of too-soft flesh,
miracle cubs, pawing at death. No one has swaddled you

tight enough to keep it out, but now the wind
wills its song from your paralytic lips—

the catch-all caws of child-fright the neighbors hear
at night, mistaken in thinking you were gone.

They remember it into the mouths of their dinners
the first time it took more than one bullet, the echo

rattling in the walls as dusk puckered into evening.
They sing along, layering their animal calls

into a bunting of sun-dried pelts, waving
over the morning when they find you in the grass, arms

gravel-scrubbed, cheeks rough as salt licks, tiny
rain clouds of warm breath still suspended above

your pied heads. Storm orphans, they make a home in you
who escaped the grip of your fathers' disappointments,

you who were spit back like words into the named world—
the chosen changelings, only a little death-bitten, only a little

wild, those snarl-cries like a hymn half-recognized.

Diorama of a Tiny Death

Beneath a paper ceiling the basement sways,
    keeps the hidden bassinet, still

lined with sloughed off skin, rustle of dry petals
    inside—mums, a residual hush,

or just the murmur of an emptied room.

It echoes up the razor-slit vents, ripples
    like wind along the nursery walls, arched

windows die-cut, one pane yet punched
    free, left hanging.
                In the corner, a mobile
of Maple helicopter pods, half pink,
    half tawny blades broke open, spilling

dead seeds from their bellies. No dolls
    in this house—only a spindle

red-dressed in thread, unraveling
    on the bed in the room next door.

I nudge the shrunken comforter,
    a patch of salvaged gauze—swish

then crunch of exoskeleton, peeking
    iridescent from beneath. My finger

jumps, but then I see—just an onion husk
    for bedding.
              Misfortune is a house
built for sibilance, and this is

where the haunted sleep, each breath a question:
    shuffle of feet, self, or nothing?

Lost Ring

Hands slicked in roof-gutter glitter—
burnt cigarette stubs and pop tabs mixed
with muck of birds and extant flora, the sky's
unsentimental jetsam—I gave up.
That's not what I was looking for, you said
when I climbed down into the word *divorce*,
your hands slowly slipping
from the ladder below.
                    Whose is the saddest
sadness, we ask for hours—mine
or ours? The ghosts on TV move their hands
through us again and again. We drowse
into them, their faraway urgency
like names from grade school we can't recall.
The knotted strings gather on our fingers;
we'll never remember to change.
Night's horizon lets itself out like a waist,
in little grudges, and we don't take each other
to the roof to drink or smoke or eat.
What did we think would happen
to all the things that fell from our hands
up there?
                    We gray into a next day. Untouched,
the lost ring dozes in its sluiced cradle
of maple veins and cigarette paper.

Poem in Which I Play the Cheat

                                    I could explain
that when he touched my arm, a field opened
inside me, so I lay down there like a stunned doe
wedding herself to the ground for its green.

But you should understand it began before that—

Sun as first love: when I was small,
I would close my eyes each afternoon
and press myself into its heat, so much
like a body, a welcome weight on top of me.
Its light split my skin, and I opened
to the infinite red and shine beneath my lids
as time thickened and pleasure oozed
like syrup into the bowl of my skull.

What I mean is that I fall in love with surfaces—

When I touched his arm, the horizon flickered
before us, and I knew the sky was only
a scratched film of sky. I fixed on its sun nonetheless,
wanting until a kind of night fell in my chest.

Self-portrait in Imalone, Wisconsin

In the rustic delirium of the plains,
            it's sun from everyangle, and guilt
is kaleidoscopic as disease, doubling
            in the eye trained on unbroken landscape—
this canopy of breath between sky and wheat.
            I have huddled in it for centuries,
hemming my arms' reach, sealing my edges
            with the steel chill of the sink.
In halfmoonlight I shed my petal breasts
            onto the floor with no one
to see me sweep them up each morning.
            Glacial indifference moves through,
calving whole faceswaistshands from my mind.
            But some nights, the children I left
at home still crawl into the pit of me.
            They sift through black heaps
of memory like deadwheat, braiding regrets
            into the most delicate jewelry.
Husk-crowned, I am the saddest queen.
            This is how we wake to our winters:
cradling only the face we don't recognize.
            And yet I can't say who I'd like to be
is any different from who I am. You see,
            in my halfheart is a pair of mirrors
that stare at each other, and between them
            is a self even I am not allowed to see.
Once, a man came through and combed me
            for stories. Look, I told him,
it's a boringtale we are always telling:
            how our failings become dwellings—
the only ones we can never run from,
            little cankers we live in.

Dorothy in the Desert

The sky behind you is a sherbet
pastiche of movie set hues:
violet dunes on the horizon's
spread of tangerine, the sunset
just a blood thread
where the world is halved
by the lingering dusk
into the day that's passed
and the coming night. Nothing
is easy as that, Aunt Em
said as you left. Your friends
have gone now, too, satisfied
by platitudes about love
and courage and brains. See
how far those got you. As far
as you can see, the grown world
is empty. *Lost* is the word you try,
but when you open your mouth,
language rolls down your chin
like cud, splintered with shreds
of unfamiliar syllables. You wanted
to be only your own. Didn't you.
If a word falls in the desert,
does it make a place to stay? Here,
only the night's indigo wraps
around you, a listless cloud.
Under a rind of moon, the silver dog
endlessly digs a hole in the sand
for your voice to sink into.

Apricots

In Ohio's sky, there is no ocean blue to hope for. Its only reflection is the electric hue of television screens, a constant beam of light beneath. But it's blue nonetheless—an aerial pool of fisheye reflections: cobalt bed posts, flickering crystal vases, and blue-jeaned children scattered like flotsam across azure living rooms.

We never had a TV, so my mother thought it was a shade too blue to be true, this sky. Our house was all browns and peaches and grays and greens—the color of handmade things. My father was obsessed with green—grass, yes, but also emeralds, limes, snakes, peas, parakeets. He filled the rooms of our house with these objects until we were squeezed out, forced to sleep on the lawn: my father, my mother, my sister, and I lying in a row, straight as green beans. The parakeets circled all night. Once the house had split its seams, spilling rotten apples and dead geckos onto the sidewalk, my mother packed us up and left him. She said the quest for something greener had eaten his mind.

Cut loose, we found ourselves buoyant and free as kites. The three of us drifted to unfathomed altitudes. Our new house was so high up on a hill that we seemed to be living in the sky. From up there, we could hear the world rushing through us just like water, and it all seemed suddenly manageable, so we decided to stay. My mother painted every wall and ceiling and floor a different shade of blue, and the empty rooms were so enormous that their edges looked to me like horizon lines. We spent entire days watching one another from miles away. Bloated with sky, we lived like reflections of the happy families below—and in this way we stayed afloat, quickly forgetting the earth and colors other than blue.

But secretly, I knew there ought to be another color for things like zucchini or bees or blood or apricots. I remembered apricots, though my sister told me I was wrong—that things like apricots were gone. Still, I pretended to eat them, gnashing my teeth at the painted clouds on our ceiling, chewing through our slate-colored days, swallowing whole swaths of blue. The world, I learned, tastes nothing like it should. This was our undoing.

I gulped down so much that our sky began to shrink. Our huge rooms collapsed one by one until we had nothing but a single closet left. It had been painted a deep navy, so being inside felt like settling into a permanent midnight. We lived like that for a long time, the three of us pressed against one another in there—backbone to backbone, shoulder to kneecap, ear to clavicle—like a lost constellation up on the hill, our limbs twisted into the shape of a poorly patched ship filling up with blue.

Accident, Maryland

Self-portrait in Accident, Maryland

Nothing can be left to luck for us.
In a town like this, one only slips
      into love as into a noose—my mother's
breakneck marriages warned me. Fools,
      we built a home here anyway,
settling on the shifting dunes of youth.
      Nightly, the river sneaks from its bed
just to crawl beneath our sheets
      and touch us like a tender drunk.
Black water cradles our porcelain heads.
      Every morning we walk a tightrope
from the bedroom to the kitchen,
      each year the twine a little thinner.
Over burnt waffles, we weep
      into the electrical outlets, driven
in our fear of loneliness to kiss
      the wall's slicked socket-lips.
Some evenings, our bones break in place
      of bread at the dinner table
as the dunes around us collapse
      in the greedy hands of the river.
We reconsider each other. Our voices
      rise as the sky falls and rights
all night in the frame of our window.
      How can we leave if the world
outside is just a shoddy cardboard prop?
      My mother's old foible turns
fable once I find a lesson in the slack
      of the softest rope, our love
a rough tongue at my neck, and you
      like a stool beneath me:
it's not an accident—this perpetual itch
      in my clumsy foot to kick.

Poem in Which I Play the Wife

And yonder all before us lie / Deserts of vast eternity.
—Andrew Marvell

After the honeymoon, we strung my libido up
with twine and hung it over the kitchen sink to dry
next to the rose saved from our first date—
but the libido stayed stubborn-soft and moist.

Next we boiled my libido with tongs, then
bleached it, starched it, and slipped in two collar stays.
I wore it to work with a pencil skirt, a real win.
In time I outgrew it (my husband said he knew it)
and left work after popping too many buttons.

Once the kids came, we put my libido in a jar
with a twig and poked three holes in the lid,
but it made no noise and lay very still
in direct light, so they soon lost interest.

Years later, we found it floating in the pool,
so we fished it out with a six-foot skimmer.
We laid it on the lawn and rubbed it down
with Lysol, then kept it like a quarter
in my car's center console, where it rattled
incessantly, my libido keeping us up all night.

Tired and tense and feeling rather over it,
we buried my libido in the garden. Underground,
it swelled to twice its normal size and sprouted
up from the earth like a yellow squash,
which deeply embarrassed my husband.
So we peeled it and pared it julienne style,
then finally ate it with a seared tenderloin.

Self-portrait in Between, Georgia

In Between, one finds our field of empty eyelids,
our orchard of four-fingered hands, split
trunks and, climbing them, our slew of awkward kids,
not quite anything
yet. We are never
twenty-six in Between—only
halfway to twenty-seven,
or five quarters past twenty-five.

The children in Between don't feel
strongly. They wish. They wash. They lack
conviction. But one could say, their grandmothers
remind each other, they are going places.

In Between, our infants turn
like clock hands in their sleep, grape toes
grazing wooden pegs, ticking crib bar
to crib bar.
          They refuse empty spaces
and the settlement of limbs, deadly
and comfortable as even numbers.

In the hour after copper pupils emerge
in the yard, and before the green street
lamps click off below our bedroom windows,
Between's mothers dream. We have only
ever wanted to get to This, Georgia,
or the lesser known That.
Often, we are caught
for days in the gloom of our waking.

Poem in Which I Play the Sideshow

Tempting, I know—the white kabob of fire,
the dazzling salad of glass, the sword
poised to be poured down this happy hatch—
all the things you could put in a mouth

but don't. Well I do—and I have two,
if you want the truth: one for each house
like a kissing booth, both shuttered now.

Who doesn't want it both ways? A siren-saint.
So it was currency, this crock—an act of girl,
not god. Love was a blade I could eat any day—

two at a time seemed easy. I took them
in vanity, watching myself as if
from across the room, amused.

Eventually, the inevitable: they stuck.
There I was, propped doubly open and singing,
my throat split, my face a peeled lily.
Oh—regret, the crowd whispered.

You see why sealing my lips
to one was out of the question—call it
staying true.   I did want to.

No Place (Dorothy Remembers)

Out here the din of tin on tin hangs
just below an orphaned smudge of cumulus,
threatening fickle weather.
The particular maliciousness of rain

in winter says: consider what you'd do
for a dollar—consider skin; consider it
penance for the runaway's sin, the problem
of the absconding heart. Consider it

gone. You know home as a word
worn through, like your name, threadbare
version of you. At dawn your cowardly
companion tells you the dog is missing.

They always come back, he says. Don't
let him fool you. With the past
like a pistol at your back,
anyone can be brave. In Kansas,

the bent back of your aunt mirrors the sickle.
She's threshing herself down
to the thinnest husk, her longing
now just a paper kernel.

Inheritance

You return
and find the door has been waiting for your key,
which sings as you fumble it, clinks
in your palm like jostling baby teeth.

Draped in your mother's satin, the bedroom is a casket
wired with light bulbs, an interview.

The phone snores in its cradle
and startles when you touch it, says
don't mistake this house for your own.

But the voices of your parents stew
in a crock-pot on the kitchen counter.
How long has it been on?
How tender
they must be by now, just murmurs,
falling off the bone.

Don't even open the door to your old room—the world
in there won't know you.

This is how a house ends: once emptied,
the walls erode as the wind picks up,
and you are left
coaxing your memory back like a dog.

Relentless

My father was a mime. Always waving his arms at us. Always drawing lines. Even in sleep, his nervous hands pressed and pulled the air like dough. Sometimes my mother woke to an O, his mouth like a hurricane's eye, eerily quiet inside.

At the dinner table, he usually just spooned silence to his lips, leaving the butter to melt down to a lake in the crater at the center of the mountain of my mother's mashed potatoes on his plate. Relentless, his invisible knife. The dog drooled, hypnotized.

During our evenings in the family room, he would build himself into a man-sized box and then spend hours jiggling an invisible key in its lock. Once he got in, he fondled its corners and gazed at the forbidden space outside its walls, where the rest of us played checkers and watched TV. Often, he stayed in there all night.

One morning we came downstairs to find him sitting on the ground, back straight, head slumped down, leaning on air. His fingers were vaguely blue, and he was shivering, as if it was cold in the house. It was then we knew he'd finally locked himself out.

Some Oz

Sowing Ohio

Housebound in this town, love yellows.
Stay, and watch the walls peel away
from their ceilings.
        Look through this window:
        a mother stretches herself, and pulls
        at the roof, little blanket feigning escape.

Her sallow skin is a singed letter
rescued from a fire.
        Behind her
    in Sunday dresses, two daughters bend,
    hinged at the middle, and spend
    hours scouring the curry-colored rug—
        something lost, a button popped.

Their dark hair's turned tawny,
        the color of searching too long,
        color of color gone.

        A miniature twister turns itself dizzy
        and blows figure eights through the room.

Husks, the daughters ripple
and tip, then pick themselves up again.

        The walls flutter as the long-armed mother
        holds them.
            Upstairs, a father is whispering,
            I want to live, forever
            climbing out the window.

See how easily it all comes down—

how quickly the table kicks off its legs;
      how the light bulbs drop
            into the yellow sea of carpeting;
how the blinds break apart
             and scatter like leaves;
how the house only wants to shake
      itself down to a fistful of seeds
            cast wide across its square lot of wheat.

Recurrence

Fluorescence washes the room,
drenches us—the dark-haired girls,

and wells electric in the cups and spoons
on the rug between us. Always, our heads

are laced with braids, our faces gone
soft as dough in our hands. We watch

the walls droop around us, tired of waiting.
On the sofa a mother sits and tugs

at her lips, stiff with a lifetime of patience.
Limestone by now, they crumble in her fingertips.

In another house a man whisper-sweeps
our names beneath his kitchen floor

and stacks photos like sweaters
too small, folded into a drawer.

He wrings his hands over the linoleum,
and moonlight trickles out of them.

Sometimes he appears at our door,
candescent with apology. A flame in his throat

illumines his skin, translucent as a jellyfish.
Thousands of words branch like nerves inside him,

and we read them all, searching for our names,
finding only gibberish. How slippery

he is, always coming back like this.

Diorama of a Funeral

I pour a salt solution into the shoebox, enough
       to float the whole chrysanthemum rigmarole:

rubber bouncy balls—my aunts like buoys
       in a sea of black felt,
                 draped like mourning
frocks on the kitchen's tiled horizon,
       where my mother drags her dinghy of hope—
           an old birthday balloon, poked through.

I smear some ink beneath her eyes,
       and pull her into the living room, where a tide

of grackles rises and falls,
                confetti at the window.

I shred my grandfather's tissue fingers—
       a fluttering deafness, and construct
           a tree of twigs to mimic a hand behind him.

The plastic pastor roofs our doll-sized guilt
       with two webbed hands,
                 the blessing missing.
I tip the baby's empty cradle, forbidden, dripping
       prayer beads as the metronome plays the role

of our gold-gilt clock, clucking its old tongue
       at a toppled Barbie—little sister sleeping.

Later, I will move her tiny feet though the dark box,
       trap dawn's infant breaths under netted fog,

and finger-trace a father's name,
                the crack that spreads
       across the scene's fourth wall, invisible.

Some Oz
for a father

We stand at the top of the Miamisburg Mound
overlooking the industrial district, a stacked complex

of glistening roofs and chain-link stapled onto the plains.
You want photos of the coming funnel clouds

as they birth themselves. You want to be close
enough to grab the tail of one like a bridle

and ride it into another life. You are dreaming
of *The Wizard of Oz* cyclone scene—the lunatic

chickens blind-weaving through dirt, the tumbleweed
limbs of uncles blowing into the cellar

as the mares bolt for one lick of life unsaddled
before the end, and the twister bends

like a finger in the distance, beckoning.
You are remembering how you envied their abandon

the day you watched your mother divide
pennies from dimes from baby teeth

and let the difference determine how many
counties away the next storm would fly her

from that place. But your father beat her to it,
his cement-dipped boots left on the porch for years,

sequined with mill rust—a sad-pageant shrine,
reminder to wake into your life, lest you lose yourself

to the dream of a sparkling city, or a heart
still clanging inside a steel man.

I am thinking of a postcard you sent me
from the Aviation Museum: *You know how they flew*

those old planes? Big as boats, but it was all
in the slope—aerodynamics.

Carve yourself a wing from the shale of this place,
you wrote—*something to fly you out*

of the black basin of old age. You sent that one
from the road, our runaway, storm-chasing.

I'm embellishing again. Those postcards were never sent,
and you didn't have to travel to find disaster.

You just wanted to be alone with your ache.
I've been thinking it wasn't the rush of storms

so much as your love for them—from the first time
you scooped the wind onto your tongue

and swallowed as much as your tiny body could hold:
that sweet smelling air that parents a stillness

you knew in the womb, the murky drown and dazzle
of debris among the astral billows, swimming

flecks of metal trailer roofs like confetti, the faceted glare
like an infant memory of the world before it settled

in your eyes. Even before you saw one, you dreamt
its hollow center, you said—a self you recognized.

You were mesmerized by its blind anger and promises
of change in the boot-scraped landscape

of western Ohio. Where else could it take you?
Almost a decade away—and you might have remained

on the ground only as a shadow in spin, dropping
the occasional postcard to us from that far funnel

you lived in, hoping to be tossed into some Oz,
where your mother and sisters were

all thin stalks of beautiful skin, unhusked
by time, your father still alive.

Some Oz where the clock of your life could unwind.
But you've returned to us now, your hands

full of years like salvage. And how could you
have known what you'd wake to—a home

inescapable, you wearing your father's face.
Here on the mound, I understand you

feel impossibly heavy, your mind a foundry of regrets
as you search for a word like an opening

into some storm strong enough to take us both
to a place where your daughters can forgive you.

The Stove Tender

stands beneath the mill's slatted vents, striated
with slate shadows. Head up, the bone colored
morning cups his pupils. Palm cradling the lever,
he thrusts his gloved fist forward, dropping
a god-sized claw into the pit,

                             bright as a star's eye,
extracting from it solid light. Just above the mouth
of a man-made volcano, one can suspend a life
spent peering down its throat,

                             pulling up hot metal
tongues, wordless from the babbling furnace,
where steel is forged from white flame in orange
sheets, electric with heat, a fluorescent premonition
of rust—the color of its end, the same as its birth.

The Miami River Floods
for a father

Over the barkeep, the TV floats like a satellite, spinning
the flood as one of our many ends. Downtown, the Miami River

lifts from a buckled bed to lie in the rust-pocked arms
of its city. We consider the myths to be made from coincidence:

how many babies will be born tonight in heroic backseat
deliveries as cars float down the freeway? They will carry

those stories all their lives like everyone else—
not from memory, but narrative inheritance. How dutifully

we gulp down circumstance as fate. I imagine
you came to my mother as an airborne body to flight—in fits

of fear before you learned to hold your weight upright,
to steady your chest while death's quick breaths pumped through

your throat in shots of rum—the constant threat of life
upending. The sewers' song flows into the bar. *I can hear*

the river rising, I say, mistaking the sound of water
for a vessel it runs from. *Marriage was my downfall*, you insist,

and I don't tell you that my mother dowsed for joy
beneath the pyre of her life after you, never divining

how many ways a world could end. In poem
after poem, I have let floods and cyclones carry you away.

The truth is you left on two feet. Or the two of you split,
a simple decision. I once wrote that your own father escaped

home in a hailstorm, driving his Ford off the road. He did
believe heaven to be falling once or twice, according to some.

What of the rest? He died from heart disease or cancer.
And what of the disaster at hand? *Thales thought water birthed*

   the universe, I say, amateur philosopher of crises—
and so our bodies are mostly water, twin to their origin.

   I can't help but believe you are stamped inside me,
and I'm afraid of my home—its mirrors, its dependence. We leave

   the bar to walk, but find the fractured face of the sky
in the brimming street—an optical trick I can't quite believe,

   though flotsam circles and dives just like birds,
acting out the lie. It is a weak excuse for flight—

   this family mythology. I submerge my feet,
unwilling to wait for the water to recede.

Blood Loop

My daughter's penchant for theft formed as a mirror to mine—a genetic marker, like identically crooked noses or dimpled chins. As a child, I took everything that spoke to me: the cat's stuffed mice, the neighbor's tulips, single hairs from my brother's head. Though I'd refused my mother's breast as an infant, years later I pushed my sister's cheek aside to get her milk—I never had an interest in things given freely. Scoldings only whet me, and the loot got bigger as I aged: bikes, cars, boys. You could even say I stole my daughter from her father. I simply slipped a hand in his pocket when he wasn't looking and shook out the promise of a daughter into a little cup. A secret seed.

In the womb, she bled me dry, and I knew I'd passed on my filching gene. No pile of food was big enough, no pitcher of water tall enough, no night of sleep satisfying. In a blood loop, her hunger danced with mine: the more I gave her, the more she wanted from me. I grew skinny and sallow, only my belly swelling from my hips like a blister. For months my heart startled and clenched, feeling the tug of her thirst. Sometimes I could hear a soft sucking sound in the middle of the night, then a self-satisfied cooing loud enough to match the locusts outside.

I'm not ashamed to tell you I sucked right back. Fasting worked at first, but eventually temptation took over. So I bit a hole in the loop: after each meal, I would sit very still for an hour, then run around the neighborhood all night, burning through the food before she could. Other times, I would just reach down my throat and pull it all back up. For the rest of the pregnancy, she became my little backup battery. Her energy surged through me. Charged, I saw magenta behind my eyes.

She weighed less than three pounds when she was born—late, mind you. They dragged her out breech and had to pry her little mouth like a leech from between my legs. Both fists full of placenta. After that, her hands were always full of something that wasn't hers: rubies from my ears, purse straps in church, dolls from the playground. Can you believe I found myself telling her to give them back? She'd stolen from me the joy of taking.

I decided to reinvest myself in this passion, starting at home. One day I went looking for quarters in her room and I found her baby teeth in a pill case—four little pearls plucked from my jewelry box. I tucked them into my palm, and when I turned to leave, she appeared in the doorway holding my mother's never-bequeathed engagement ring. There we stood, stuck in a shame loop: lady see, lady do—the two of us blushing in tandem like siren lights.

Honesty, Ohio

Self-portrait in Miracle, Kentucky

Home is a bullet I swallow again and again, hoping
to emerge unbroken from where I've been: trapped
in houses that fall like people—perpetually
into themselves, becoming a heap of near-misses
from which I rise, saying *God, I made it*:

                    even as an infant
swaddled in smoke and blinking at the stunned police
while they marvel at the gray lace of a burnt cigarette
spread across my chest like a blessing or a pyre
pitched on a mound of mistakes:

                including the man
whose arm lifts from my memory to aim a kitten
like a dart at the wall, one hand on the pipe in his lap,
deep laughs stewing in his drawl as I try to evaporate:
from my best friends' fates,

           girls who never stop descending
the stairs between two men, their backs growing smaller
like balloons let drift above: me as a boy flicks salty water
from my cheek after he's begged to finish in me, not waiting
for an answer heard over his hounds' bellowing:

                     a dirge
I sing from memory as I spoon a dust ground from poison
roots into my tea, calling *no-name, my no-name*
to the little sponge in my belly:

           so it's only my own cry
that ascends the day I see a baby sleeping in the hollow
of a tire on a friend's driveway and there are so many
colored pills blinking inside me like Christmas lights
that I think *is it mine:*

          the same question I ask the day
my cousin ODs and her terrier tries for hours to bark
the dead leaves back into their trees, as if we can return
to ourselves so easily, the miraculous on command:

                    as if
it's all been a magic trick, I suddenly wake at the snap
of the dog's jaw, rubbing my eyes—not saved, I realize,
but changed:

         like the magician's trembling rabbit suspended
before the crowd, *I made it:* from an empty grave, a girl.

Born Again

It was the year of miracles
piling up inside you, tiny
and black as chokeberries.
One: your parakeet, deceased
but still wriggling in his shoebox
in the garage, feathers threaded
with white, nervous with worms.
Two: your cousin's arm,
making its home in the dirt
somewhere across the world
as he dozed in your twin bed,
lopsided with bandaging,
the fan breathing a dance
into his one empty sleeve.
Three: your mother's eyeball
in the casket, peeking white
from beneath her stone
eyelid, unglued—a wink. How
easily it could have been
a prank to you then. How easily
she could have risen, beaming
as you all bawled her name
in vain. And finally: the little egg
of rage you sat in, a yolk
the summer would incubate
until the day you were born from it
under a canopy of hands
as the pastor wept and pulled
the devil from your belly like a fish
caught in the grip of his tongue's
Hallelujah. Hallelujah, they said.

Dorothy's Funnel

The spurned sky purples
and throbs

with last night's voices, pitched
into the black

now caught in the violet gauze
of morning

like resin smudges, suspended
cherry bombs

and a girl, halved

by the shadow of a silo
climbs down

from a roof, climbs
rib by rib

into the pit of herself.
The ground

many-mouthed, opens
its cellar doors

and crowds of moths,
tattered tongues

stumble out
stunned

by the light, violently
bright, brighter

than they could have fathomed.

Self-portrait in Story, Wyoming

Ever the aimless cowgirl, I ride
the highest horse I can find, dragging
my high heels like training wheels behind.
Would you believe me if I told you

I've married twice and divorced
sixteen times? Sixteen spurs
line my two feet, anklet of shame
on the left, pride on the right.

My kids pepper the plains
like cattle herding in lines
that spell out all of my names
in script seen only from a plane

I've piloted all my life. A lesson
in Western confession: Story
is the curtain I work behind. Listen—

in my ribs, I've lassoed and fenced
all the women I've been. I swear
they have never ceased
to believe they exist.

Poem in Which I Play the Subject

The Poet is at it again—stripping me down, taking
slate to my kitchen knives, punching out windows
in my childhood home—all means, no end.

Tonight She's brought with her a boy—I know
the one. Only wanted a bit of *fun*. In the basement,
She's given him all my clothes, and they tremble

in his hands while I stand naked on the page.
I know I'll never get them back, not inside
this perpetual present tense, this fence
around the dogs of adolescence—how they beg

to be let go. Does the tragedy even matter? Better
if I am a metaphor, maybe: some kids trapped
in a burning apartment, while the Poet is a fireman

rescuing tiny flames instead. How tenderly
She cradles each one through the doorway, her little
raisons d'être. Anything to save the Poem, She says.

The Language of Daughters

builds a daughter's house: beams of *I* like fingers accuse
each other in circular rooms, circuited with silent vowels
that string themselves together endlessly.
                                    Some words
are composed entirely of silence, and these will trickle out
of a daughter's mouth as she sleeps.
                                    Of course, certain gradients
of daughterbreath won't translate: fear of fathers, fevers, regret.

There are sixty-seven terms for red, forty-two for leaving,
but none for sorry.
                    Unwatched, a daughter's verbs switch tense,
a life unbecoming as *was* swallows *am* swallows *will.*
                                    With age
the language falls away like scurf from a daughter's brain,
but when it is heard again, her dumb tongue burns
with voiceless consonants:
                    tk tk of fingernails on drywall,
sh sh of lace on tile, *st st* of silver trembling in its drawer.
Her mind
            is blanched in a bowl of light—her lips part,
her body stutters, she loses a ribbon of time.
                                    Syntax splinters
with words unlearned, and hidden roofs collapse inside,
leaving only interjection—O
                        a daughter's life is spent
sifting the wreckage of meaning heaped between her teeth.

Self-portrait in Honesty, Ohio

It was a lie—my claim I'd never stood
in a wheat field, never held an ear of corn,
the slippery white kernels like buttons
between eager fingers.

In honesty, Ohio, I'm sorry I said that.
I'm sorry I told you I'd never be back.
I'm sorry I claimed I saw only gray
bones of pavement under rust-licked faces.

In Honesty, Ohio, I was born on a tilled plot
of my mother's corn-fed sorrow, harvested
and suckled by yellow funnels of wind.

And in Honesty, Ohio, there was a wheat field,
sharp with empty stalks, soft with fingers.
In honesty, there were many.

I had put them all away, but lately
I've been combing through them at night.
I braid their brittle sheaths, finding more
and more of them empty.
Some crumble in my hands—
that's how sorry I am.

Acknowledgments

American Literary Review: "In Which I Play the Cheat" as "On
   Adultery"
Arts & Letters: "The Stove Tender"
The Adroit Journal: "The Language of Daughters"
The Collagist: "Blood Loop," "Self-portrait in Hurt, Virginia," "Self-
   portrait in Between, Georgia," "Poem in Which I Play the
   Runaway" (Reprinted in *Best New Poets 2013*)
Crab Orchard Review: "Self-portrait in Only, Tennessee," "Infants of the
   Field," "Some Oz" (Reprinted in *New Poetry from the Midwest*)
Dorothy Sargent Rosenberg Prize site: "Self-portrait in Honesty, Ohio"
   (as "Confession")
Fairy Tale Review: "No Place (Dorothy Reconsiders)," "Dorothy and
   Uncle Henry," "Dorothy and the Lone Ranger," "Letter from Aunt
   Em," "Dorothy in the Desert"
The Florida Review: "Self-portrait in Miracle, Kentucky," "Self-portrait
   in Imalone, Wisconsin"
Grist: the Journal for Writers: "Diorama of a Fire," "Neverstill, Oregon"
   (as "Tinnitus")
Harpur Palate: "Self-portrait in Accident, Maryland"
Jabberwock Review: "Music Box"
Kenyon Review Online (KROnline): "Diorama of a Funeral," "Diorama
   of a Tiny Death"
Linebreak: "Self-portrait in Needmore, Indiana"
Meridian: "Self-portrait in Last Chance, California"
Midwestern Gothic: "Halfhearted" and "Apricots"
NANO Fiction: "Relentless"
PANK Magazine Online: "Self-portrait in Aimwell, Alabama," "Born
   Again," "Lost Ring," "The Miami River Floods"
Pittsburgh Poetry Review: "Poem in Which I Play the Wife" as "Wife's
   Fable"
Portland Review: "Dorothy Tries"
RHINO Poetry: "Self-portrait in Nightmute, Alaska"
This Land Press: "Sowing Ohio"
Winter Tangerine Review: "Poem in Which I Play the Subject" as "The
   Post-confessional Poet"
Versal: "Bad Luck" (Reprinted in *LitRagger* and *Paragraph*)

This book exists because of support and advice from many people, including my family and friends. I offer my endless gratitude to Doug Diesenhaus for his love and wisdom. Thanks to the poets who have given me feedback and insight on this manuscript: Ariana Nadia Nash, Linwood Rumney, Jamie Lalonde-Pinkston, Emily Skaja, and Caitlin Doyle. Thanks also to Don Bogen, as well as those in workshops at UNC Wilmington, the Hinge, and University of Cincinnati. Thanks to Writers in the Heartland, Wildacres, the Dorothy Sargent Rosenberg Fund, and *Crab Orchard Review* for their generous support. Finally, I want to thank Richard Blanco for believing in this book, as well as Peter Covino, Sarah Kruse, and everyone at Barrow Street for making it possible.

Rochelle Hurt is also the author of *The Rusted City*, a collection of prose poetry and verse published in the Marie Alexander Series from White Pine Press (2014). Her work has been included in *Best New Poets 2013* and she's been awarded literary prizes from *Crab Orchard Review*, *Arts & Letters*, *Hunger Mountain*, and *Poetry International*. Her poetry, fiction, and creative nonfiction have also appeared in journals like *Crazyhorse*, *Black Warrior Review*, and *The Southeast Review*. She holds an MFA from UNC Wilmington and is currently a PhD candidate at the University of Cincinnati.

BARROW STREET POETRY